"A gentle story of the importance of seeking help when family members and others around the child may be struggling. *The Island* supports children who may feel alone, encouraging them to reach out for kindness and support."

Hephzibah Kaplan, Art Therapist, Director of London Art Therapy Centre

"This sensitively written and delightfully illustrated book will reassure young children, who are isolated by living with a parent with a mental health problem, that it is not their fault nor their job to fix a parent's illness. It opens up a dialogue for a child to acknowledge a range of emotions that they may be experiencing."

Janey Treharne, Jigsaw, South East

"*The Island* sensitively depicts the isolation and loneliness a child may feel living with a parent with depression. The story allows for discussion with the child to explore their caring role and the self-blame felt by children who have a lived experience of parental mental health. The story gives a powerful message, encouraging a child to share their experiences and opening up conversations about this difficult subject."

Sarah-Jane Farr, Family Support Keyworker, Early Help WSCC

"The power of these stories lies in their deeper natural and archetypal metaphor, something like the deeper Mother Earth continuity below any surface. Before even reading any of these *Therapeutic Fairy Tales*, you feel their tenderness through the stunningly beautiful illustrations."

Molly Wolfe, Art Psychotherapist, Sandplay Specialist

The Island

This beautifully illustrated and sensitive storybook is designed to be used therapeutically by professionals and caregivers supporting children with a parent who is suffering from depression. With engaging, gentle and colourful illustrations that can be used to prompt conversation, it tells the story of a Girl who is helped to feel less isolated from her parent's depression.

This book is also available to buy as part of the *Therapeutic Fairy Tales* set. *Therapeutic Fairy Tales* is a series of short modern tales dedicated to exploring challenging life situations that might be faced by children. Each short story is designed to be used by professionals and parents as they use stories therapeutically to support children's mental and emotional health.

Other books in the series include:

- *Storybook Manual: Introduction To Working With Storybooks Therapeutically And Creatively*
- *The Night Crossing: A Lullaby For Children On Life's Last Journey*
- *The Storm: For Children Growing Through Parents' Separation*

Designed to be used with children aged 6 and above, each story has an accompanying online resource offering therapeutic prompts and creative exercises to support the practitioner. These resources can also be adapted for wider use with siblings and other family members.

The Island – part of the *Therapeutic Fairy Tales* series – is born out of a creative collaboration between Pia Jones and Sarah Pimenta.

Pia Jones is an author, workshop facilitator and UKCP integrative arts psychotherapist who trained at The Institute for Arts in Therapy & Education. Pia has worked with children and adults in a variety of school, health and community settings. Core to her practice is using arts and story as support during times of loss, transition and change, giving a TEDx talk on the subject. She was Story Director on artgym's award-winning film documentary, 'The Moving Theatre,' where puppetry brought to life real stories of people's migrations. Pia also designed the 'Sometimes I Feel' story cards, a Speechmark therapeutic resource to support children with their feelings. You can view her work at www.silverowlartstherapy.com

Sarah Pimenta is an experienced artist, workshop facilitator and lecturer in creativity. Her specialist art form is print-making, and her creative practice has brought texture, colour and emotion into a variety of environments, both in the UK and abroad. Sarah has over 20 years' experience of designing and delivering creative, high-quality art workshops in over 250 schools, diverse communities and public venues, including the British Library, V&A, NESTA, Oval House and many charities. Her work is often described as art with therapeutic intent, and she is skilled in working with adults and children who have access issues and complex needs. Sarah is known as Social Fabric, www.social-fabric.co.uk

Both Pia and Sarah hope these *Therapeutic Fairy Tales* open up conversations that enable children and families' own stories and feelings to be seen and heard.

Therapeutic Fairy Tales

Pia Jones and Sarah Pimenta

978-0-367-25108-6

This unique therapeutic book series includes a range of beautifully illustrated and sensitively written fairy tales to support children who are experiencing trauma, distress and challenging experiences, as well as a manual designed to support the therapeutic use of story.

Titles in the series include:

Storybook Manual: An Introduction To Working With Storybooks Therapeutically And Creatively
978-0-367-49117-8

The Night Crossing: A Lullaby For Children On Life's Last Journey
978-0-367-49120-8

The Island: For Children With A Parent Living With Depression
978-0-367-49198-7

The Storm: For Children Growing Through Parents' Separation
978-0-367-49196-3

The Island

For Children With A Parent Living With Depression

Pia Jones and Sarah Pimenta

Routledge
Taylor & Francis Group

LONDON AND NEW YORK

First published 2021
by Routledge
2 Park Square, Milton Park, Abingdon, Oxon OX14 4RN

and by Routledge
52 Vanderbilt Avenue, New York, NY 10017

Routledge is an imprint of the Taylor & Francis Group, an informa business

© 2021 Pia Jones and Sarah Pimenta

British Library Cataloguing-in-Publication Data
A catalogue record for this book is available from the British Library

Library of Congress Cataloging-in-Publication Data
Names: Jones, Pia, author. | Pimenta, Sarah, illustrator.
Title: The island : for children with a parent living with depression / Pia Jones and Sarah Pimenta.
Description: Abingdon, Oxon ; New York, NY : Routledge, 2020. | Series: Therapeutic fairy tales | Summary: A grateful turtle repays a Girl's kindness by helping her feel less isolated by her mother's depression. Includes a note on how to use the book as a therapeutic resource.
Identifiers: LCCN 2020001473 (print) | LCCN 2020001474 (ebook) | ISBN 9780367492007 (hbk) | ISBN 9780367491987 (pbk) | ISBN 9781003044994 (ebk)
Subjects: CYAC: Depression, Mental--Fiction. | Mothers and daughters--Fiction.
Classification: LCC PZ7.1.J726 Is 2020 (print) | LCC PZ7.1.J726 (ebook) | DDC [E]--dc23
LC record available at https://lccn.loc.gov/2020001473
LC ebook record available at https://lccn.loc.gov/2020001474

ISBN: 978-0-367-49198-7 (pbk)
ISBN: 978-1-003-04499-4 (ebk)

Typeset in Calibri and Antitled
by Servis Filmsetting, Stockport, Cheshire

Visit the eResources: www.routledge.com/9780367491987

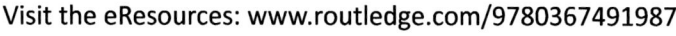

Acknowledgements

A special thank you to Stuart Lynch for all the time and creative support he generously gave to *The Island*. Thanks to Hephzibah Kaplan for her enriching input and ideas.

Thanks to Speechmark for looking after our fairy tales so well and turning them into such beautiful books. A special mention to our editor, Katrina Hulme-Cross, for her calm, steady guidance, and enthusiastic support for these stories. And to Leah Burton, Cathy Henderson and Alison Jones for taking our books into production with such care and attention.

Thanks to all the other people who have supported us along the journey: Alastair Bailey, Tamsin Cooke, Katrina Hillkirk, Molly Wolfe, Fiamma Ceccomori-Jones, Sarah Farr, Annie Duarte, Jacob Pimenta-Richardson, Antonella Mancini, Daniele Ceccomori and Alex Poole.

A word of caution

Before starting *The Island*, please take a moment to read below

The Island has been especially written for children with parents living with depression and mental health difficulties. The storybook is designed to serve as a therapeutic resource to support children with their personal, emotional journeys, to generate discussion and reflection alongside an adult reader.

Given the sensitive subject matter, it is essential the story is read in the right setting, with respect and due care for the child's well-being, leaving plenty of time for reactions, feelings and thoughts. This is not a story that can be rushed.

For the adult reader, professional or non-professional, it is advisable to read this story first alone, to ensure you have time to process your emotions in order to prepare for therapeutic work with your child reader.

For extra resources on how to work with this story, and examples of creative exercises, please go to the online resources: www.routledge.com/9780367491987. For ideas on how to work with story and image in general, please refer to our *Storybook Manual: An Introduction To Working With Storybooks Therapeutically And Creatively*: www.routledge.com/9780367491178.

Once upon a time there was a young Girl who lived on an island with her Mum. It was a small, steep island, with spiky mountains and thick forests. Sea-fog rolled in, so the air was soggy. Dotted around the island were many rocks. Boats had to take care not to crash.

The Girl didn't much like this island. If it was hard to leave, it was even harder to visit. More than anything, the Girl didn't like the way this island made her Mum feel. Often, her Mum wouldn't want to leave the house. In the mornings, her Mum took ages to wake up. While she slept, the Girl would search for flowers outside to put in their kitchen. When her Mum arrived for breakfast, looking red-eyed and puffy-faced, it was like she hadn't slept at all.

"Morning," said the Girl, putting on her brightest smile. "I've made the fire … and a pot of coffee. We have flowers too. Look, aren't they lovely?"

"Ah, yes," sighed her Mum, sinking into a chair, a dark-blue shawl around her shoulders.

The Girl had arranged the flowers in a tall glass, but her Mum didn't seem quite able to notice.

"Do you want to come outside with me, go for a walk?" asked the Girl, smiling even harder as she poured out coffee.

"Not today," said her Mum and frowned briefly at the window and the rolling fog outside.

The Girl watched her Mum's gaze fall into her cup of coffee as if she'd lost something at its bottom.

"You could come outside with me," said the Girl gently as she laid out a bowl and spoon on the table for her Mum. "We could meet someone ... a friend?"

A shadow crossed her Mum's face, "So many questions and this bad weather ... it's tiring me out."

"I'm sorry," answered the Girl quietly, eyes falling to the floor.

"You go," said her Mum after a while. "Remember, don't speak to strangers."

"No, no, I won't. Mum, I'll be out for the day ... I'll bring you some more flowers. See you later."

The Girl stepped out of the house and stared back at its closed door, her heart squeezed tight. It was a mystery why her Mum did not want to come outside today or any other day. Was it something she'd said? As she walked away, her mind tied itself in knots.

Mum, oh Mum, what have I done?

Heavy-footed, the Girl followed a path to the shore.

Worn out from all her thinking, she chose to sit on the nearest big rock. Salt-water pooled around her. As she narrowed her eyes and stared at the sea, she could just make out the mainland, its faint, blurry shape in the distance. A sudden rush of feeling took the Girl off guard, making her eyes well up. A stream of tears dripped off her nose. Time passed until the Girl's watery gaze was caught by something floating nearby.

The Girl breathed in sharply, her body turning still. It must be an old fisherman's net, she thought, with something caught in it. Leaning out as far as she dared, the Girl grabbed a corner. The net was heavy as she pulled it in. To her surprise, a round head with a pointed beak stared back at her with glistening, ancient eyes.

"Oh, a turtle, you're trapped, poor thing," she cried, blinking fast. "Let me help you."

Using her fingers deftly to unknot the net, it didn't take the Girl long to free the Turtle but instead of swimming away, it slid up the rock to join her.

It was a giant sea-turtle, the largest she'd ever seen, with soft hues of blue, green, yellow, a hint of pink, on its beautiful shell.

"Thank you," said the Turtle and the Girl clutched her knees, so she didn't fall off the rock.

She blinked in disbelief at this strange talking creature, its beak and dark eyes, long flippers and shell whose colours seemed to shift and move.

"Who, er, what are you?" she said sharply, remembering what her Mum had said about not speaking to strangers.

"You freed me," said the Turtle, "so now I will offer you something in return."

"Er ... what do you mean?" said the Girl warily.

"Three questions," said the Turtle, eyes glittering. "Ask me any three questions. I will answer them and tell you the one Truth for each. Nothing is as precious as the Truth."

The Girl's mouth dropped open, her heart beating fast.

"Why isn't my Mum happy?" she blurted.

Just the act of saying it aloud, made the Girl's cheeks burn. She could not believe the world was still standing. The Turtle closed its eyes for a few seconds, before opening them.

"Your Mum's happiness is not to do with you," sighed the Turtle. "None of this is your fault."

A cool breeze rose, lifting the fog. The Girl swallowed a desperate sob, "Can anyone help her?"

"Yes," said the Turtle soberly, "but it can't be you … you are a child and you have a child's life to live."

There was a gust of wind. The sea-fog was thinning. The Girl drew in a breath for her third and last question, when the Turtle held up a long fin.

"Wait," it called out, "the last question … it must be for you … you must ask it for you."

With a frown, the Girl hesitated, glancing across at the mainland, its outline the clearest she'd seen.

"How do *I* get off this island?" she asked carefully.

The Turtle nodded, "On the North shore, by a tall forked tree, is a rocky point ... beyond lies a causeway where the tide goes out twice a day. The causeway links the island with the mainland."

The Girl's face brightened. She knew this tree, she'd seen it from afar, but the Turtle hadn't finished, "The path is open to everyone … but each person, the first time … they must walk it alone."

Dropping her rucksack, the Girl stared at the Turtle, her eyes dark as coals. She felt her heart crack. *Mum*.

"You can come back and go freely," said the Turtle firmly, "but this first time you must go alone. Come now, I'll take you there before the tide turns, and then I must leave you."

With a long flipper, the Turtle invited the Girl to take her place on its giant shell. The fog had almost disappeared now. Carried along by the Turtle on the crest of waves, the Girl felt a rush of feeling. There were new birds and trees along the shoreline she'd never seen before.

"Thank you," she cried, once they reached the rocky point. As she dismounted and ran towards the causeway, the Turtle watched and wished her well on her way.

Climbing up onto the rocky point, she hesitated. The causeway lay below. Heart aching, the Girl took a first step. Water lapped at the stone slabs, but it felt solid underfoot.

"Mum," she whispered into the wind, "I'm going … I'll be back, but I have to go now."

With one last glance back, the Girl broke into a run.

Wind ruffled her hair. The sun had broken out and warmed her skin. As the Girl ran, her heart pounded and she felt energy flow through her. She didn't stop until she reached the other side ... the mainland.

People, that was her first thought. So many people, old and young. They sat on the grass, walked along paths, but they were talking, all talking. As she scrambled to join them, they turned towards her. At first, she couldn't bear their curious stares.

Don't talk to strangers, she remembered her Mum's wise advice.

But when she saw one face, a face filled with kindness and something else … concern, the Girl bent down to pluck some flowers, clasping them to her chest.

"I'm here to ask for help," she said, stepping forward, "some help *for me*."